LOOMINGS
OVER THE SUET

Glen Baxter

BLOOMSBURY

THANKS TO
Jaco Groot & Henny Vrienten for technical advice on
Bavarian customs and Tofu production
Liz Calder for the loan of her Palanquin
Polly Napper for her unstinting efforts in Guildford, Yuma and Thurrock
Professor Norman Hewitt for permission to quote from his seminal work
"Snoods & Their Magnetic Fields 1926—31"
and to Katherine Greenwood for bringing the trireme round to an
elegant, impressive full-stop.

First Published 2004

Copyright 2004 by Glen Baxter

The moral right of the author has been asserted

Bloomsbury Publishing Plc,
38 Soho Square, London W1D 3HB

ISBN 0 7475 7524 X
10 9 8 7 6 5 4 3 2 1

All papers used by Bloomsbury Publishing are natural, recyclable products made from
wood grown in sustainable, well-managed forests. The manufacturing processes
conform to the environmental regulations of the country of origin.

Printed in Italy by ArteGrafica Spa

IN THE TINY VILLAGE OF LOWER
DIMCHESTER, THE ANNUAL GENERAL
MEETING OF THE CROCHET SOCIETY
BEGINS WITH A KEYNOTE SPEECH
BY LADY LUCINDA BARTLEY.

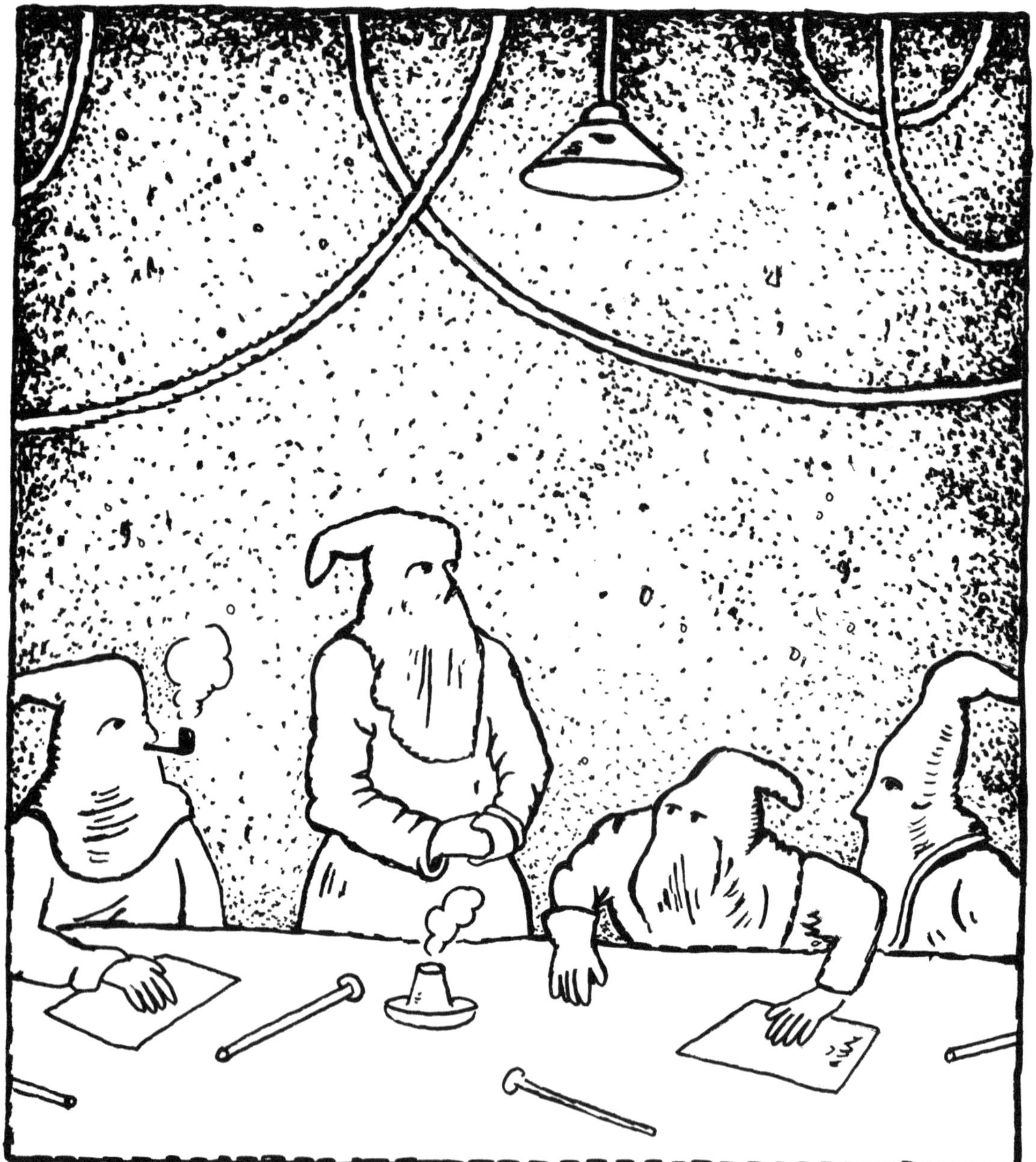

"ΤΙΠΟΤΑ ΔΕΝ ΥΠΑΡΧΕΙ!"

BUT AT THAT PRECISE MOMENT
IN THE DERELICT BARN OPPOSITE
THE VILLAGE HALL, A POLICE
INFORMER TURNS A DIAL ON HIS
HIDDEN TRANSMITTER.

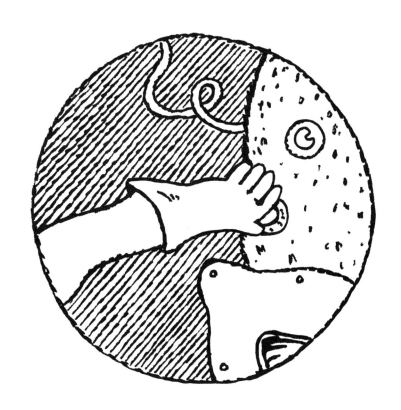

TWO WOODEN PLANKS SLIDE APART
TO REVEAL AN INDONESIAN GONG
AND A SMALL YET SIGNIFICANT
SUPPLY OF CHEESE AND TOMATO
SANDWICHES.
A RUSTED
METAL BALL
DROPS ONTO
THE FLOOR AND
ROLLS SLOWLY UP TO A
PAINTED WHITE CIRCLE ON
A BLACK SLATE PANEL
UNDER THE BARN DOOR.

DETECTIVE INSPECTOR ROBERT
LAZENBY IS INFORMED.

HE REACTS IMMEDIATELY.

THE ILLICIT SANDWICHES

ARE QUICKLY HIDDEN

AND THE ENTIRE COUNTY
CONSTABULARY PUT ON STANDBY.

15 MILES SOUTH OF INTERSTATE 8
YUMA, ARIZONA, THERE IS A
SUDDEN MOVEMENT.

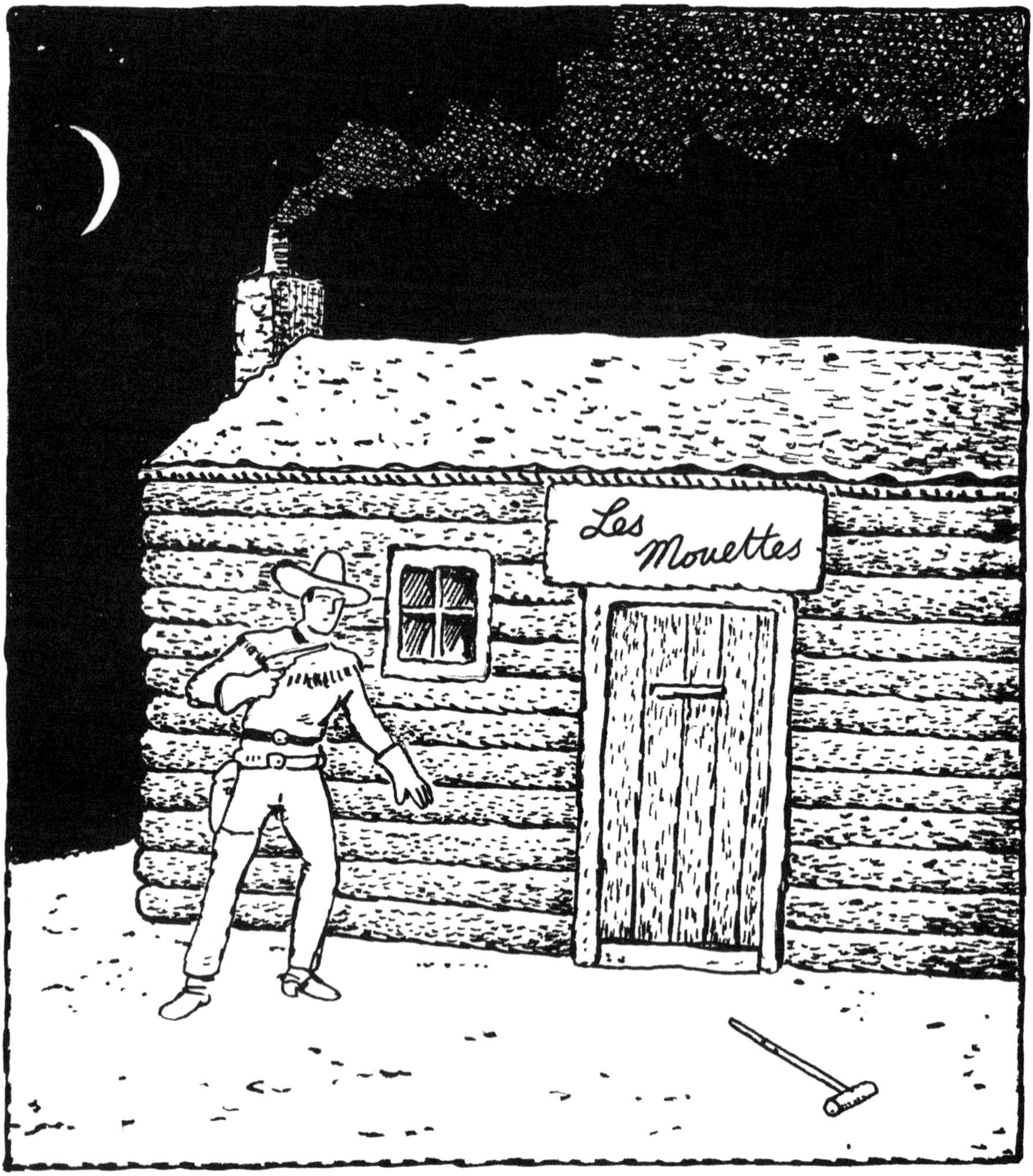
Les Mouettes

ALL IS NOT WELL

AND A GAME OF INDOOR CROQUET
IS ENDED SOMEWHAT ABRUPTLY.

HIGH ON A RIDGE BEHIND THE
CABIN, DARK FORCES ARE STIRRING.

SHERIFF McCULLOUGH RIDES
OUT TO INVESTIGATE.

A CURSORY SEARCH OF THE CABIN
REVEALS A NUMBER

OF INCRIMINATING ITEMS,

WHICH LEADS SHERIFF M^{c}CULLOUGH
TO ONE INESCAPABLE CONCLUSION:

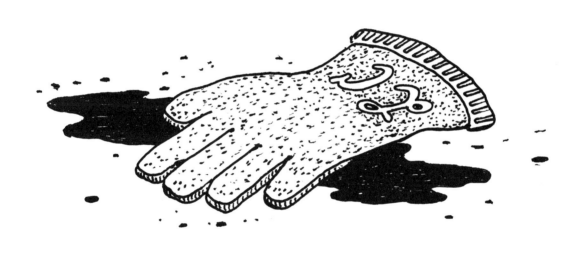

THAT THE ENGLISH SCHOOLTEACHER
LUCY HENDERSON IS IMPLICATED.

TWELVE YEARS EARLIER...

LUCY HENDERSON RECEIVES
AN UNWELCOME VISITOR.

AT THE NEWLY REFURBISHED
POLICE STATION IN LOWER
DIMCHESTER, EAST SUSSEX,
DETECTIVE INSPECTOR LAZENBY
RECEIVES AN IMPORTANT MESSAGE:

"YES, WE ARE GETTING REPORTS OF
A PLUMBING PROBLEM, SIR,"
REPORTED SERGEANT McINTYRE.

WITHIN A MATTER OF HOURS, THE
STREETS ARE FILLED WITH POLICE
CONSTABLES ON THE LOOKOUT FOR
ANYONE ACTING SUSPICIOUSLY

AND ANYONE THEY SUSPECT IS

QUESTIONED AND QUICKLY ARRESTED.

THE VILLAGE POSTMAN IS DISCOVERED
IN A COMPROMISING POSITION...

AT EXACTLY THE SAME TIME AS A

MYSTERIOUS PARCEL OF RECYCLED
SUET IS DELIVERED TO № 43
CRENSHAW AVENUE.

DETECTIVE INSPECTOR LAZENBY LAUNCHES "OPERATION IRONFIST"

AND THE ENTIRE VILLAGE IS PLACED UNDER ARREST.

THE ATMOSPHERE BECOMES INCREASINGLY
TENSE. CAREFULLY AND METHODICALLY
POLICE EXPERTS GO ABOUT THEIR
RESEARCH. INCH BY INCH THE
VILLAGE IS EXAMINED FOR PRINTS
AND EVIDENCE OF MARKET GARDENING.

GRADUALLY A DISTURBING PATTERN
BEGINS TO EMERGE AND EVEN
INNOCENT-LOOKING HOUSEHOLD
OBJECTS BEGIN TO AROUSE SUSPICION.

"MIGHT I BE CORRECT IN ASSUMING
THIS TO BE A WINDOW?"
ENQUIRED CONSTABLE FITZWARREN
SOMEWHAT NERVOUSLY.

EVIDENCE IS COLLECTED,

SIFTED AND ANALYSED,

COLLATED, FILED AND DISPATCHED

TO SCOTLAND YARD FOR THOROUGH SCIENTIFIC INVESTIGATION.

13 YEARS LATER, ON ROUTE 93,

6 MILES N.E. OF GRAYLING, MICHIGAN
U.S.A. A LONELY FIGURE STUMBLES
THROUGH THE OPENING BARS OF
"SOMEWHERE OVER THE RAINBOW."

THE DAY PASSES SLOWLY
AND THE SHARP, CLEAR OUTLINES
OF THE TROMBONE SEEM TO
BLUR INTO THE DARKNESS.
A CHILL WIND FROM THE EAST
BLOWS ACROSS THE HIGHWAY,
SCATTERING LEAVES AND THE
BROKEN SHARDS OF A CRACKED
BLUE AND WHITE CERAMIC VASE.

ARNOLD BROWNSTEIN, DRIVING SOUTH

ALONG THE HIGHWAY, SUDDENLY
REALIZES HE IS IN BIG TROUBLE

AND WITH THE SITUATION RAPIDLY

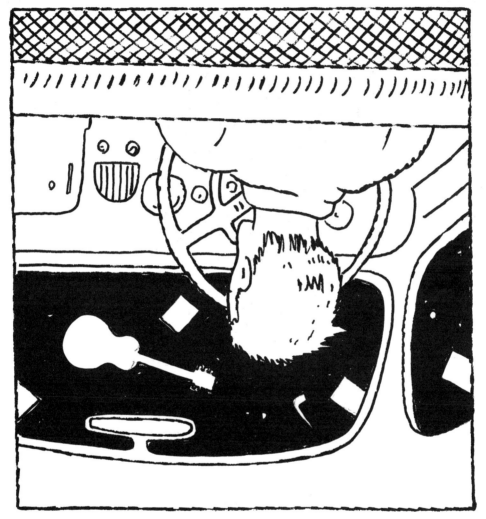

DETERIORATING, PULLS OFF THE ROAD.

TWENTY-SIX HOURS LATER
SHERIFF Mc CULLOUGH CONTINUES
HIS SEARCH FOR CLUES,

STUDYING A LUNCHBOX PURPORTING
TO HAVE BEEN USED BY HENDERSON

LESS THAN HALF A MILE AWAY, A
CRACKLE OF ELECTRICITY LIGHTS
UP A CORNER OF A BASEMENT
STOREROOM IN THE REYNOLDS
CENTRAL DEPOSITORY,

REVEALING A FIGURE SLIPPING
BETWEEN THE PACKING CRATES,

SEEMINGLY PURSUING A

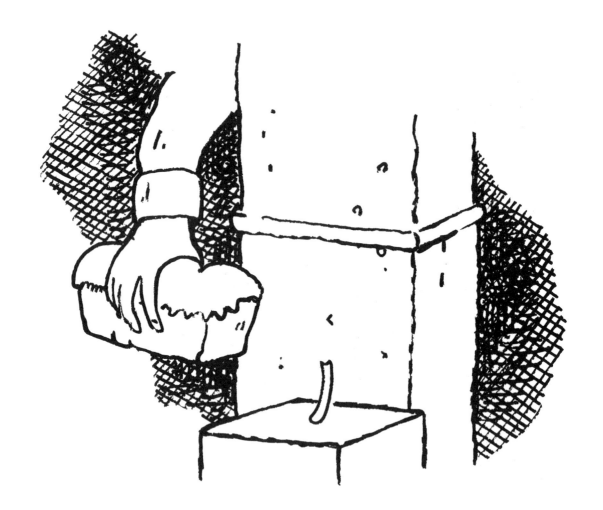

MALICIOUS AGENDA.

SIX HOURS LATER ON THE YUCATAN
PENINSULA

EVIDENCE LINKING LADY LUCINDA
BARTLEY AND LUCY HENDERSON
IS BROUGHT TO LIGHT.

LUNCHTIME, APT. 21ᴬ

MOORFIELD CRESCENT, THURROCK,

48 MINUTES EARLIER.

"ARE WE ABSOLUTELY CONVINCED
THIS IS A QUICHE, SUSAN?"

IN THE LOUNGE OF THE RED
LION INN, LOWER DIMCHESTER,

DETECTIVE INSPECTOR LAZENBY
HAS A PROBLEM.

HIS KNITWEAR FETISH HAS BECOME
THE SUBJECT OF MEDIA SPECULATION,

HIS WIFE IS ACTING STRANGELY,

AND THEIR SIX-YEAR-OLD SON JAMES
HAS DEVELOPED SOME WORRYING HABITS.

FORTUNATELY, CONSTABLE SNAIPE HAS

MANAGED TO RETAIN A FIRM GRIP ON
REALITY AS HE IS DISPATCHED ON
SURVEILLANCE DUTY OPPOSITE Nº 26
THRUMBOLD AVENUE.

8 MILES NORTH-EAST OF YUMA
A BELL RINGS AND SHELDON BRAY
HEADS OUT FOR THE SCHOOL OF
WESTERN DENTISTRY

WHERE A FLOSSING DEMONSTRATION
IS IN PROGRESS

AND THE BENEFITS OF A TOFU
DIET ARE EXPLORED IN DETAIL.

BACK IN LOWER DIMCHESTER
LADY BARTLEY DONS HER SNOOD

AND QUIETLY SLIPS THROUGH
A POLICE CHECKPOINT,

ENJOYS A QUIET LUNCH OF ROAST
CABBAGE, SQUASH AND SMOKED TOFU
IN A SECLUDED AREA OF WASTELAND
BEHIND THE NEWSAGENTS FRINGED
BY A RUINED TOPIARY HEDGE WHICH
ONCE HAD BEEN THE MAJOR TOURIST
ATTRACTION IN THE AREA AND NOW
TRAGICALLY HAS BECOME A MAGNET
FOR THOSE WITH A SINISTER AGENDA,

BEFORE CONSULTING A PSYCHIC

TO DISCUSS HER CRISIS OF IDENTITY,

UNAWARE THAT SHE IS BEING
SHADOWED BY A SENIOR OFFICER

FROM THE GUILDFORD SPECIAL
OPERATIONS BRANCH.

THERE IS A FLURRY OF ACTIVITY IN THE FACT-CHECKING DEPARTMENT

OF BULGROVE COMMODITIES IN THE MONADNOCK BUILDING, MARKET STREET, SAN FRANCISCO.

OF LUCY HENDERSON IS HANDED OVER
TO LOUIS BRADLEY, HEAD OF RESEARCH,

AND SOME STARTLING FACTS

2 oz Belgian suet

$$A + B + \blacksquare = 8 + \frac{x}{16}$$

(Lady Lucinda Bartley)

oxygen   alcohol   mayonnaise

LH

ARE BROUGHT TO LIGHT.

AT THAT PRECISE MOMENT IN THE
MAKESHIFT OPERATIONS ROOM,
LOWER DIMCHESTER,

A PATTERN BEGINS TO EMERGE
WHICH THROWS THE EVENTS IN
NORTH AND CENTRAL AMERICA
INTO SHARP RELIEF, LEAVING
DETECTIVE INSPECTOR LAZENBY
TO REACH AN INESCAPABLE
CONCLUSION.

HE BRINGS HIS TEAM TOGETHER AND

MAKES A DRAMATIC ANNOUNCEMENT:

' IT'S QUITE CLEAR WE HAVE A
SITUATION THAT SEEMS TO DEFY
ALL LOGIC. I FEAR WE HAVE NO
OTHER OPTION BUT TO SEND TWO
MEN OVER TO YUMA TO LIAISE WITH
OUR AMERICAN COLLEAGUES AND
TO CALL UPON THE SERVICES OF
AN ACKNOWLEDGED EXPERT IN
THE FIELD OF THE PARANORMAL...

... DOCTOR DAGMAR BIENOWSKI."

A BADLY DENTED TROMBONE IS HANDED IN TO RECEPTION

AT THE CASA DEL BALAM HOTEL, MERIDA, YUCATAN PENINSULA, MEXICO,

AND REPORTS OF DESECRATION OF A

CIVIC SCULPTURE REACH THE EARS OF
CARMEN PEREZ , HEAD OF HOTEL
SECURITY.

OUT IN COCHISE COUNTY, ARIZONA,

TWO OF LAZENBY'S OFFICERS
ARE MAKING AN EFFORT TO
BLEND IN WITH THE LOCALS.

THE MOOD AMONGST THE LOCAL
POPULATION THOUGH REMAINS

SCEPTICAL AND AT TIMES
DOWNRIGHT MOROSE.

HOWEVER, WITHIN HOURS OF THEIR ARRIVAL, A GRIM DISCOVERY IN A NETWORK OF CAVES SEVEN MILES EAST OF THE TOWN OF DOUGLAS CASTS A SHADOW OVER THE PROCEEDINGS.

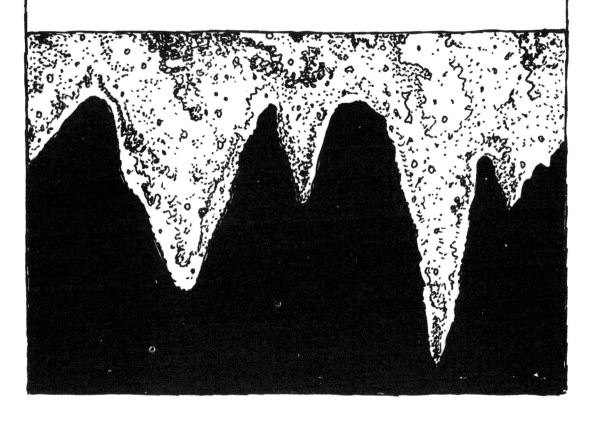

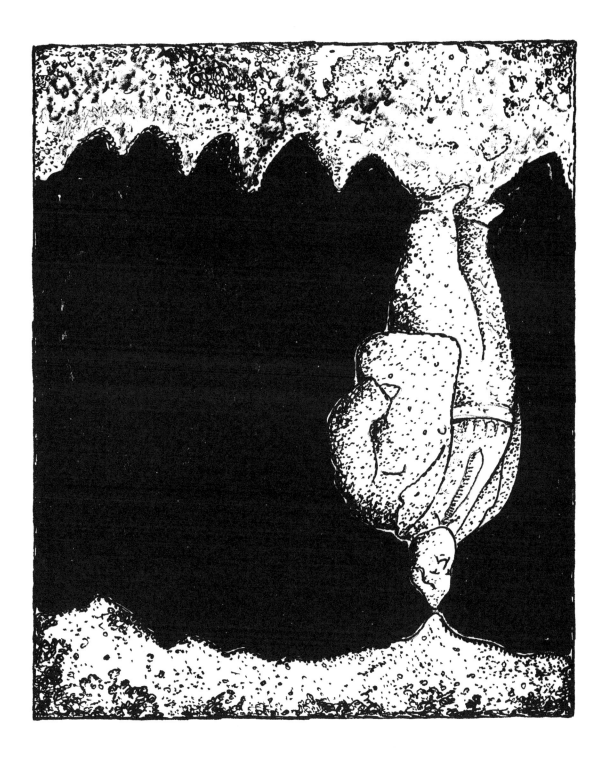

FRAGMENTS OF A PLECTRUM

AND A BLOODSTAINED NOTE
ARE DISCOVERED NEARBY.

THERE IS MOUNTING UNREST BACK
IN ENGLAND. DISTURBING NEW
REPORTS ARE LANDING ON LAZENBY'S
DESK EVERY FIFTEEN MINUTES.

IN DESPERATION HE TELEPHONES
Mc CULLOUGH. THERE IS NO REPLY.

THE SHERIFF SITS ALONE IN A
DARKENED ROOM, EDGY AND TENSE,

SEEKING SOLACE IN HIS
PUMICE COLLECTION.

JUST WHEN EVERYTHING SEEMS
TO BE GETTING OUT OF HAND

LAZENBY HAS A STROKE OF
GOOD FORTUNE.

HE LEANS FORWARD TO
QUESTION ONE MEMBER OF
THE CROCHET SOCIETY WHO
HAS DECIDED TO SPEAK OUT,

DESPITE BEING THE RECIPIENT
OF A NUMBER OF THREATS,

WARNINGS, ABUSIVE TELEPHONE
CALLS AND A BADLY DAMAGED
PARCEL OF SUET.

"LUCY WAS A TALENTED WATERCOLOURIST,

BUT SHE DID HAVE A DARKER SIDE.

THERE WERE ALWAYS RUMOURS CIRCULATING THAT HER INCOME CAME NOT FROM THE TRUST FUND SET UP BY GREAT AUNT ISABEL BUT FROM SOURCES WHICH WERE, SHALL WE SAY, NOT ENTIRELY ABOVE BOARD.

I DIDN'T BELIEVE THEM UNTIL ONE DAY I HAPPENED TO PAY AN UNANNOUNCED VISIT TO HER EMBROIDERY STUDIO

AND DISCOVERED LUCY'S
SINISTER SECRET."

ON THE SECOND FLOOR OF THE
MONADNOCK BUILDING ,LOUIS

BRADLEY IS CHECKING THROUGH
THE DOSSIER ON LUCY HENDERSON.

AS A PICTURE OF HENDERSON FAMILY
LIFE BEGINS TO EMERGE, HE READS
THE TRANSCRIPT OF A STATEMENT
GIVEN TO AN ENGLISH SECURITY
ADVISER THE PREVIOUS YEAR.

"HER YOUNGER BROTHER RICHARD
RUNS AN UNSUCCESSFUL SARDINE
FISHING BUSINESS IN NORFOLK..."

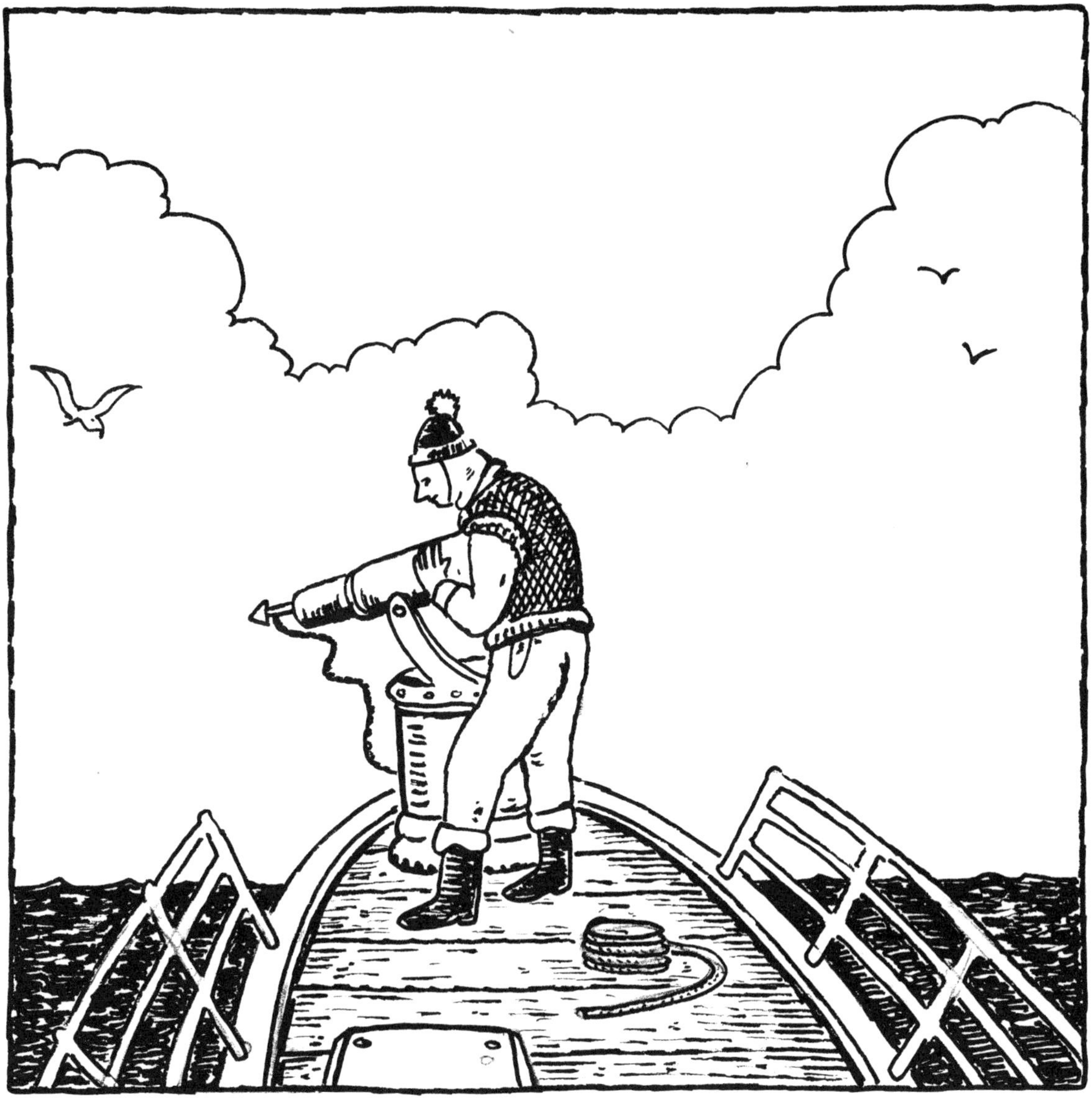

THE OLDER BROTHER NIGEL WORKS
IN THE CITY, HAS NO CRIMINAL
RECORD AND APART FROM AN
UNHEALTHY INTEREST IN
HESSIAN IS OTHERWISE
QUITE UNREMARKABLE.

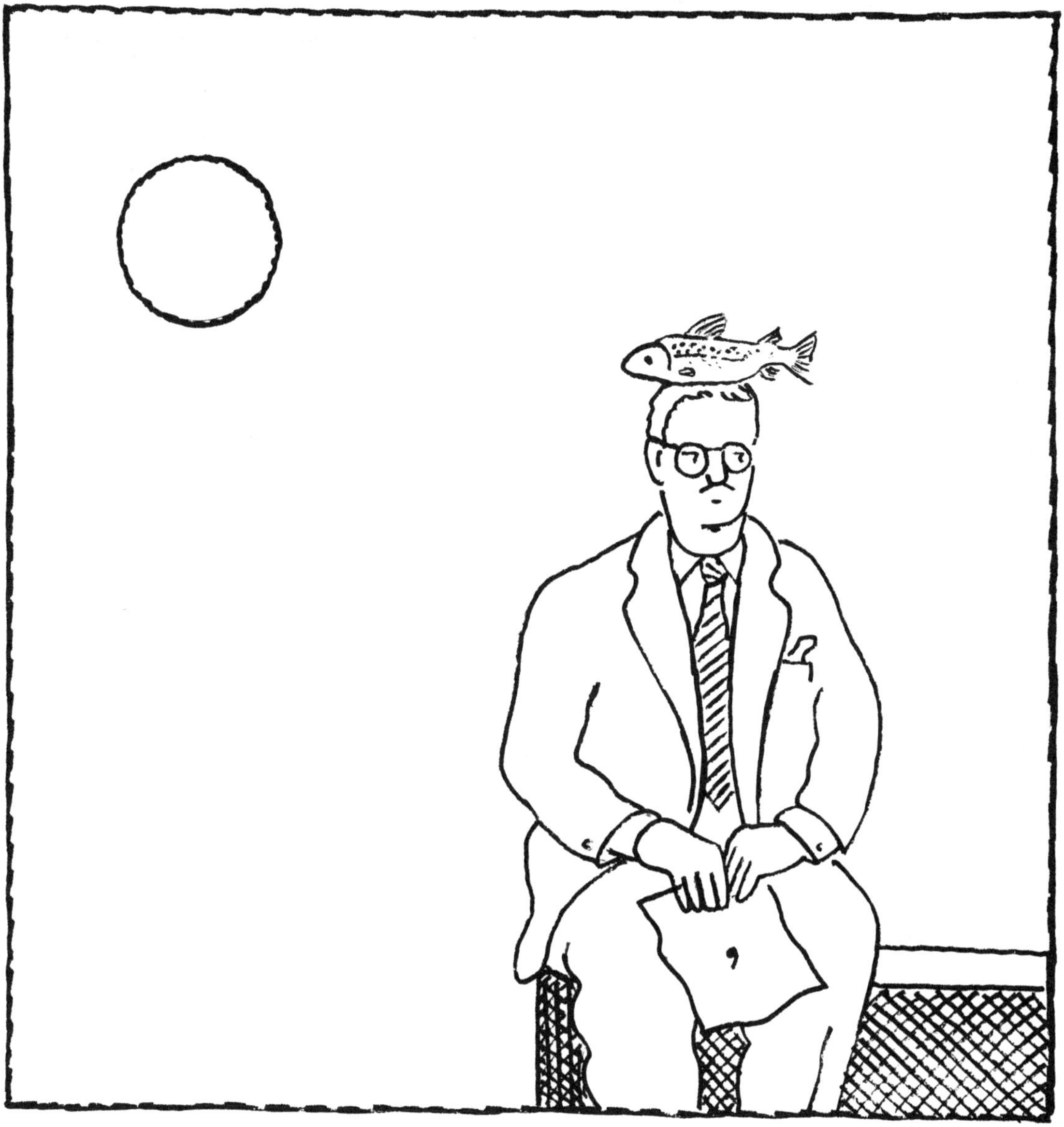

VERY LITTLE IS KNOWN ABOUT LUCY'S

MOTHER, WHO DISAPPEARED WHILST ON HOLIDAY, ONLY TO REAPPEAR TWENTY-THREE YEARS LATER AS THE OWNER OF A CHAIN OF SEEDY PORTUGUESE CASINOS.

LUCY'S FATHER, CHARLES PEREGRINE HENDERSON, A MARINE BIOLOGIST AND FORMER WORLD SCRABBLE CHAMPION, HAD A DISTINGUISHED CAREER IN MILITARY ESPIONAGE

BUT SEEMED DETERMINED UPON HIS
RETIREMENT TO CARVE OUT A NICHE
FOR HIMSELF IN THE WORLD OF
INTERNATIONAL CUISINE.

TO THIS DAY HIS RECIPE FOR EGGS
BENEDICT IS STILL FEATURED IN
"BURMESE COOKING MADE EASY".

AS THE CLOCK TICKS AWAY ON
A HAZY SATURDAY AFTERNOON
SHERIFF McCULLOUGH RECEIVES

A PACKAGE POSTMARKED
"LOWESTOFT, ENGLAND"
CONTAINING PHOTOGRAPHS AND
A TESTIMONY SIGNED BY RICHARD
HENDERSON PROCLAIMING THE
INNOCENCE OF HIS SISTER LUCY:

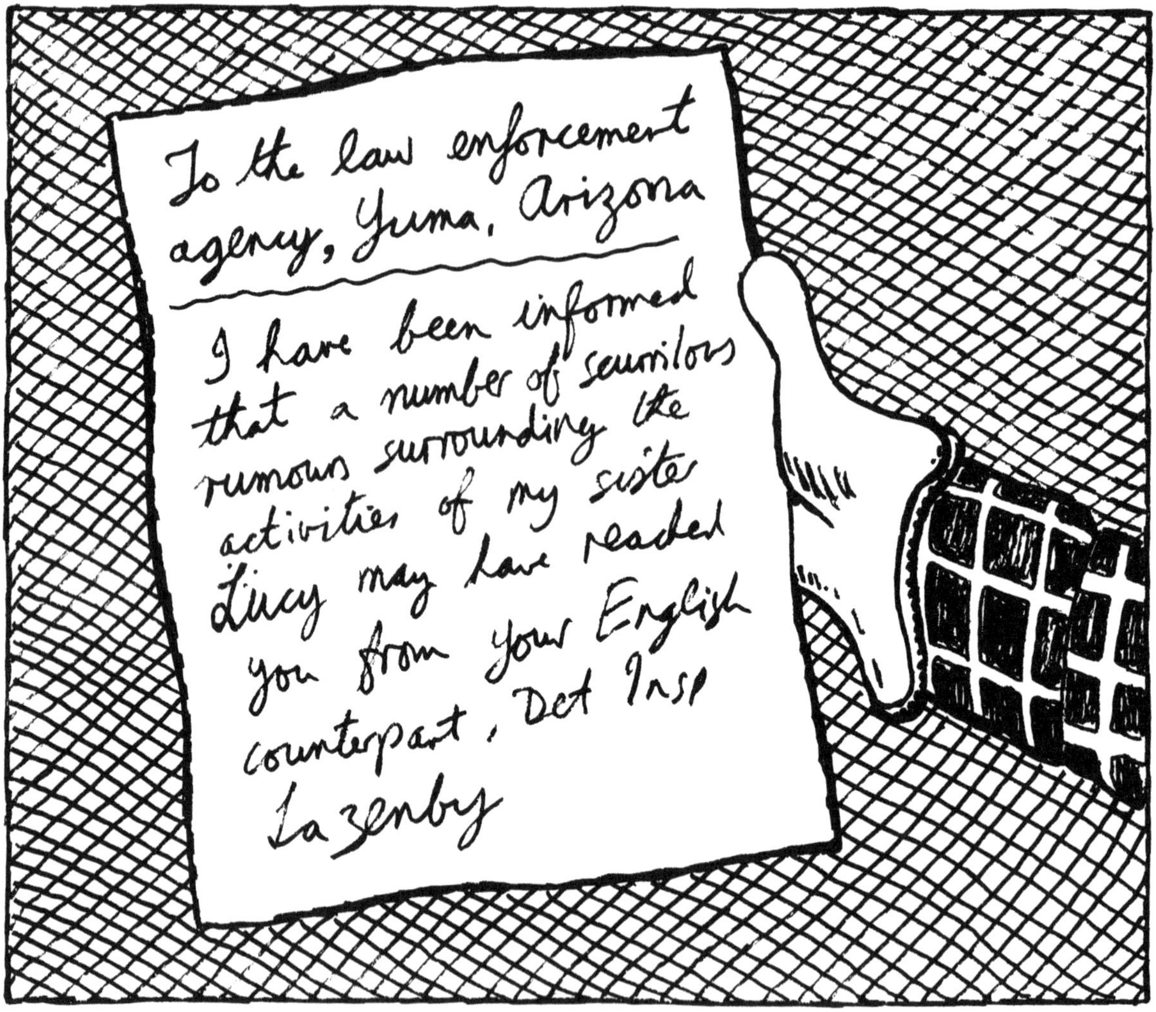
To the law enforcement agency, Yuma, Arizona
I have been informed that a number of scurrilous rumours surrounding the activities of my sister Lucy may have reached you from your English counterpart, Det Insp Lazenby

THE LETTER WENT ON TO SAY,
" THE SO-CALLED 'SINISTER SECRET'
INVOLVED NOTHING MORE SERIOUS
THAN A RADICAL NEW WAY OF
SERVING A WHOLE SALMON ON A
BED OF CORIANDER-INFUSED SUET.

—SEE EXHIBIT Ⓐ ON NEXT PAGE..."

EXHIBIT (A)

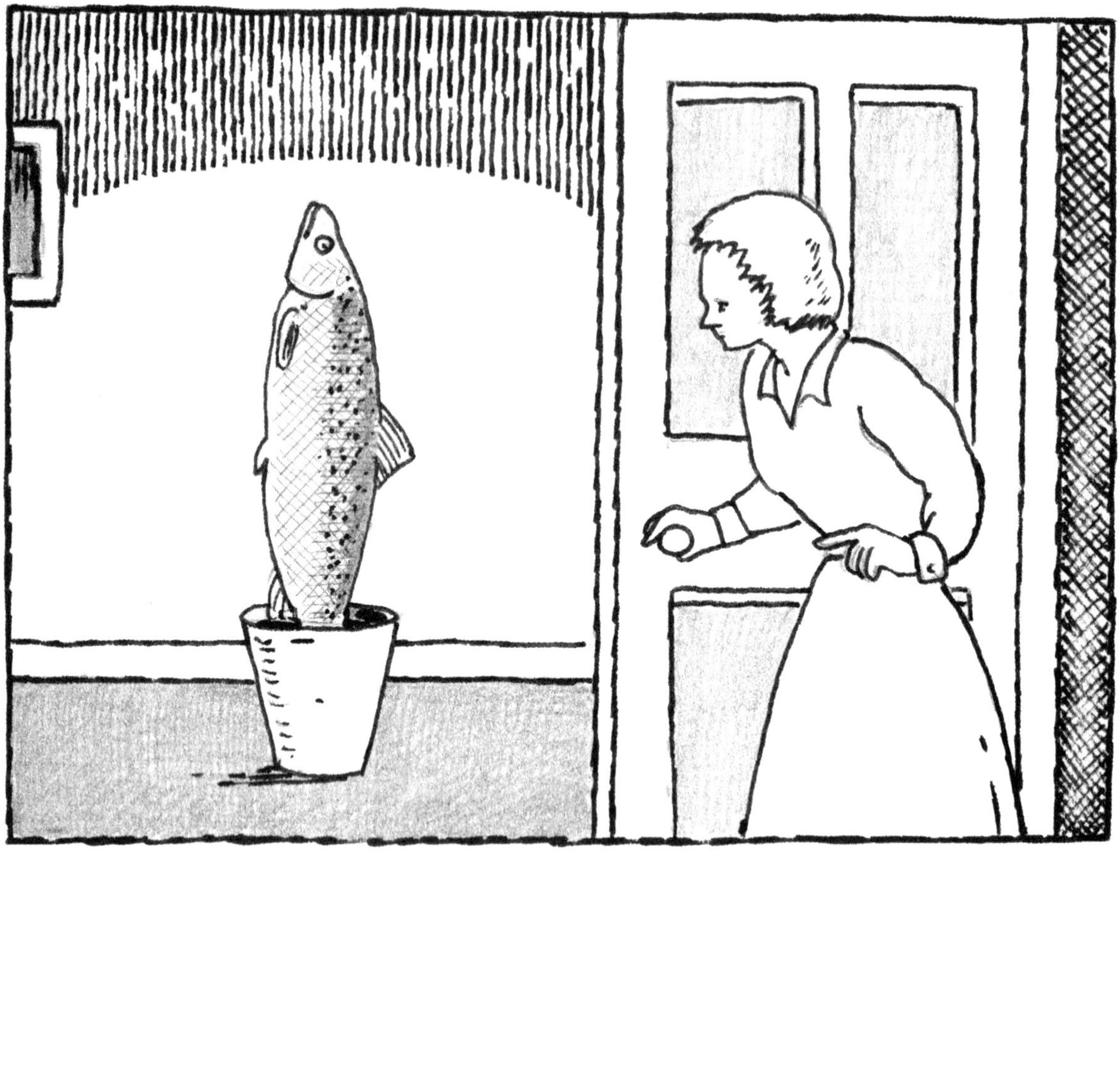

SHERIFF McCULLOUGH EXAMINED THE
CONTENTS OF THE PACKAGE BEFORE
TURNING TO HIS DEPUTY AND
SAYING,
"YOU KNOW, WAYNE, NONE OF
THIS SEEMS TO MAKE ANY
SENSE."
"I HATE TO CONTRADICT YOU, SHERIFF,
BUT I CAN SEE A PATTERN
EMERGING HERE" REPLIED THE
DEPUTY.

" JUST LOOK AT THESE MINUTE TRACES OF ORGANIC MATTER ON THE CAPITAL 'L' OF 'LUCY'... LOOKS LIKE FLECKS OF TOFU TO ME".

THE WIND WHISTLED OVERHEAD,
MASKING A FEW DISCORDANT
NOTES OF MUSIC AND, IN THE
DISTANCE, THE HOWL OF A
COYOTE.
AT THIS MOMENT, McCULLOUGH
NARROWED HIS EYES AND
LOOKED DOWN AT THE GROUND,

REALIZING FOR THE FIRST
TIME THAT THIS MIGHT JUST
BE MORE SERIOUS THAN HE
HAD AT FIRST THOUGHT.

AT THE POLICE DEPARTMENT, 113TH
PRECINCT, BAISLEY BLVD, QUEENS, N.Y.

LIEUTENANT MOCHALSKI CHECKS
THE FILE ON ENGLISH ANTIQUE
DEALER TONY ARBUTHNOT —
IMPORTER OF RARE PENAL
ARTEFACTS FROM THE NETHERLANDS,
MOST NOTABLY THE

NOTORIOUS "RIETVELD SPECIAL",

Exhibit 29ᴬ

ALLEGEDLY COMMISSIONED BY A DUTCH BENEFACTOR WITH CLOSE CONNECTIONS TO THE BOARD OF GOVERNORS AT HUNTSVILLE.

FOUR HOURS LATER, ON THE
YUCATAN PENINSULA,

SERGEANT LAFORGUE TAKES STOCK
OF THE SITUATION.

WHAT HE SEES UP ON THE WINDSWEPT
RIDGE FILLS HIM WITH A SENSE OF
DREAD AND FOREBODING.

AT THE HENDERSON RESIDENCE
IN UPPER DIMCHESTER, THE
BLISSFUL FAMILY ROUTINE IS
INTERRUPTED BY A TELEPHONE
CALL.

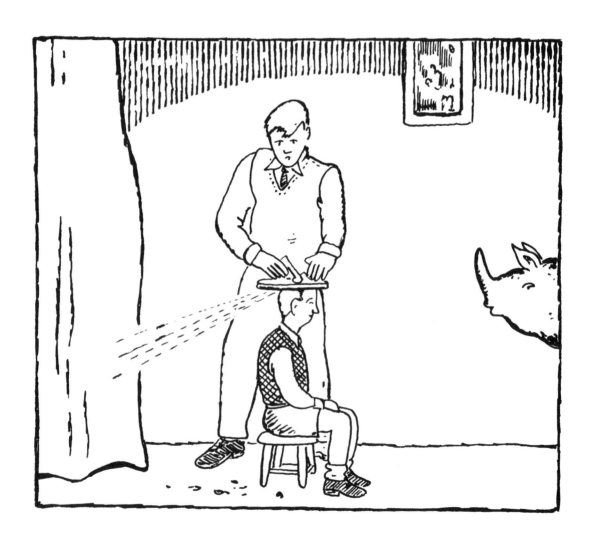

MR HENDERSON STOPS AND
PICKS UP THE RECEIVER.
"WRONG NUMBER!" HE SNAPS,
SLAMS DOWN THE 'PHONE

AND RETURNS TO HIS
PATERNAL DUTIES.

TWENTY MINUTES LATER THE 'PHONE
RINGS AGAIN. IT IS THE LOCAL
POLICE STATION.
"JUST WHAT IS YOUR CONNECTION
WITH BROGDALE LODGE, MR HENDERSON?"
RASPS SERGEANT HARDWICK.

MR HENDERSON SEEMS UNEASY.
THE TINY BLOCK OF TOFU IN HIS
LEFT HAND BEGINS TO DRIP ONTO
THE CARPET.

AT THAT PRECISE MOMENT, IN
THE GRAVEL DRIVEWAY OF Nº 149

EASTCHURCH AVENUE, FROME,

DAGMAR BIENOWSKI, SWAYING
SLIGHTLY, ANNOUNCES:

"GETTING INFORMATION. WORDS JUMBLED.
LOGDALE BRIDGE. DODGE. CONNECTOR
TO MIDDLE. TOXIC DRAW."

WITH THAT HE LOSES CONSCIOUSNESS AND CRASHES INTO THE GRAVEL. AT 151 THE CURTAINS TWITCH BRIEFLY AND A SHADOW FALLS ACROSS THE JACK VETRIANO PRINT ABOVE THE BOOKSHELF.

AN OVERPOWERING AROMA OF STALE SUET PERVADES THE GLOOM.

SITTING ALONE AT A TABLE IN "THE WHITE ORCHID", LOWER DIMCHESTER, LAZENBY IS REPEATING THE WORDS "GOONG PAD NAM PRIK PAO" TO HIMSELF. HE SCRIBBLES ON A

NAPKIN AND HANDS IT TO A WAITER.

FOUR MINUTES LATER THE WAITER
RETURNS AND ANNOUNCES:
"THE CHEF WANTS TO KNOW WHY
YOU WANT PRAWNS SERVED
IN A
MINIATURE
MODEL
OF
THE
ALHAMBRA
WITH A SIDE ORDER
OF STIR-FRIED BEAN
CURD AND PEA SHOOTS!"

LAZENBY DROPS HIS CHOPSTICKS AND RACES OUT THE DOOR

INTO THE BUSTLING STREETS, HOTLY PURSUED BY THE ENTIRE KITCHEN STAFF.

OUTSIDE THE MONADNOCK BUILDING
IN SAN FRANCISCO, LOUIS BRADLEY,
HIS EYES GLAZING OVER, IS
ATTEMPTING A FEW TENTATIVE
CHORDS,

UNAWARE THAT LADY LUCINDA BARTLEY HAS SLIPPED IN BEHIND HIM ...

WHISTLING THE OPENING BARS OF "SOMEWHERE OVER THE RAINBOW."

SECONDS LATER HE IS OUT FOR
THE COUNT AND A NUMBER OF
POTENTIALLY INCRIMINATING
FILES ARE REMOVED.

A SHADOWY FIGURE SLIPS AWAY,
MINGLING BRIEFLY WITH THE
CROWDS ON MARKET STREET
BEFORE DISAPPEARING IN THE
DIRECTION OF CHINATOWN.

FIFTEEN MILES SOUTH OF
YUMA, ARIZONA,

THE TWO ENGLISH POLICE OFFICERS
ARE GAZING UP AT THE STARS.

A BRIGHT OBJECT TRAVERSES THE
NIGHT SKY.

BOB SAUNDERS TURNS TO HIS COMPANION AND WHISPERS
"I KNOW WE'RE A LONG WAY FROM GUILDFORD, JIM, BUT THAT SURE LOOKS LIKE TOFU TO ME."
JIM, HOWEVER, IS NOT ENTIRELY CONVINCED AND TURNS HIS GAZE TOWARDS THE HORIZON WHERE A PLUME OF GREENISH SMOKE IS CURLING SLOWLY UPWARDS.

AT BANG RAK POLICE STATION, THAILAND,

KANCHIT THALAWONG AND NAKON THAKSIN ARE DISCUSSING THE LATEST REPORTS OF AN INCIDENT ON THE RATCHADAPHISEK ROAD INVOLVING A 23-YEAR-OLD MALE VICTIM, A UKELELE AND A SHORT LENGTH OF RUBBER TUBING.

TWELVE HOURS LATER IN LOWER
DIMCHESTER, THE HEAD OF CRIMINAL
INVESTIGATION AT GUILDFORD CENTRAL
HANDS OVER THE LATEST DOSSIER

TO A BEMUSED LAZENBY
WITH THE CHILLING WORDS,

"WE RAN A CHECK ON BARTLEY.
IT SEEMS SHE GREW UP ON THE
FAMILY ESTATE IN BERKSHIRE.
HER FATHER WAS A MOODY,
IMPULSIVE MAN, A LAPSED
VEGETARIAN AND A CRACK SHOT.

IT WAS CLAIMED HE ONCE
BROUGHT DOWN

18 BUTTERFLIES IN UNDER

SIX AND A HALF SECONDS.

LADY BARTLEY, ANXIOUS TO IMPRESS HER
BELOVED FATHER, ENROLLED IN THE
BERKSHIRE AMATEUR DRAMATIC AND
ARTILLERY SOCIETY AND IT WAS NOT
TOO LONG BEFORE SHE WAS MAKING
A NAME FOR HERSELF, BREAKING ALL
SORTS OF RECORDS ACROSS EVERY
COUNTY IN ENGLAND. IT WAS ON ONE
SUCH EXPEDITION THAT WE THINK
SHE CAME INTO CONTACT WITH LUCY
HENDERSON.
WE HAVE CREDIBLE EVIDENCE THAT
THE MEETING TOOK PLACE ON THE
NORTH YORKSHIRE MOORS AS

LADY BARTLEY WAS ATTEMPTING
TO BREAK ANOTHER RECORD."

CONSTABLE "WOBBLY" WILKINS LEANS FORWARD AND ANNOUNCES:
" I THINK WE CAN SAFELY SAY THAT WE ARE DEALING WITH TWO PEOPLE WHO HAVE GONE BEYOND THE BOUNDS OF COMMON DECENCY HERE."

IN THEIR TINY APARTMENT ON
ELMHURST AVENUE, QUEENS, N.Y.,

THE GROENLIND TWINS ARE
MORE THAN USUALLY AGITATED.

THEY HAVE
JUST RECEIVED A 'PHONE CALL
FROM SOMEONE ON THE WEST
COAST PURPORTING TO BE LADY
BARTLEY.
AS THE COLOUR DRAINS FROM
THEIR FACES THE TWO MEN
SHUFFLE TOWARDS THE
DOOR AND OUT INTO THE
STREET,

TO GIVE THEMSELVES UP TO
THE POLICE AUTHORITIES.

SIX HOURS LATER, AT THE 113TH PRECINCT ON BAISLEY BLVD., A TRIUMPHANT MOCHALSKI IS ON THE 'PHONE TO DETECTIVE INSPECTOR LAZENBY. HE IS HOLDING WHAT LOOKS LIKE A TINY GREEN GOURD IN HIS HAND, WHICH OCCASIONALLY HE TOSSES UP INTO THE AIR.
"I THINK WE CAN SAFELY SAY THE NET IS CLOSING NOW, EH LAZENBY, DON'T YOU?"
THE GREEN OBJECT FALLS PAST HIS OUTSTRETCHED PALM, HITS THE FLOOR AND ROLLS SLOWLY TOWARDS THE DOOR.

NEWS OF THE ARREST OF THE TWINS IS FLASHED

ROUND THE WORLD

AND IN SOME QUARTERS
THE DISTRESS IS ALL
TOO APPARENT.

THE REVERBERATIONS EVEN MANAGE
TO REACH DAGMAR BIENOWSKI, WHO
IS PURSUING HIS OWN LINE OF
ENQUIRY

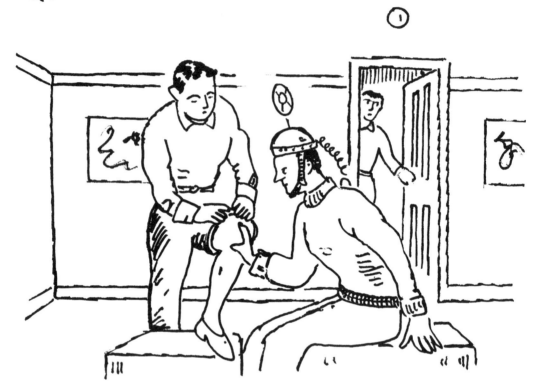

ON THE OUTSKIRTS OF DAGENHAM.

120

BACK IN ARIZONA, HOWEVER, THERE IS A QUIET AIR OF DESPERATION AS SHERIFF McCULLOUGH TRIES HARD TO MAKE SENSE OF THE UNFOLDING EVENTS.

THERE ARE CONTINUING REPORTS OF UGLY INCIDENTS TAKING PLACE IN BROAD DAYLIGHT,

LEADING TO SERIOUS DOUBTS
ABOUT THE ABILITY OF THE LAW
-ENFORCEMENT AGENTS TO
MAINTAIN PUBLIC ORDER,

A FACT HASTILY DENIED BY A
SPOKESPERSON ON NETWORK
TELEVISION LATER THAT DAY.

OVER AT BANG RAK POLICE
STATION A POWER CUT HAS LEFT
KANCHIT THALAWONG IN THE
DARK. HE HAS MISSED LUNCH

AND IS AWAITING NEWS FROM
THE FORENSIC LAB WHILST
REPORTS OF FURTHER INCIDENTS
CONTINUE TO FLOOD IN WITH
DEPRESSINGLY REGULARITY.

ON THE RATCHADAPHISEK ROAD

NAKON THAKSIN IS SEARCHING THE
CRIME SCENE FOR CLUES,

UNAWARE THAT HIS EVERY MOVE
IS BEING MONITORED FROM AN
ABANDONED SCOTTISH RESTAURANT.

SUDDENLY THE THAI DETECTIVE STOPS
IN HIS TRACKS. HE LOOKS DOWN

AND NOTICES A CHARRED FRAGMENT
OF NEWSPAPER IN THE DUST.

"BROGDALE **LODGE**?" EXPLODES LAZENBY.

CONSTABLE "WOBBLY" WILKINS
SWAYS BACK AND ANNOUNCES:

129

"YES - THOSE TWO WORDS KEPT CROPPING UP ON THE BIENOWSKI TAPES SO WE CHECKED ON GOOGLE AND BROGDALE LODGE IS AN EXCLUSIVE RETREAT ON DRINGEMOOR. THE OWNERS ARE LUCY HENDERSON AND LADY BARTLEY-OH. AND THIS JUST CAME THROUGH..."

LAZENBY SLUMPS FORWARD ONTO HIS DESK.

AS DUSK FALLS OVER BROGDALE
LODGE, A SACK IS DROPPED INTO

THE MURKY WATERS OF THE
LAKE AND A FIGURE DRESSED
AS A VICAR ROWS SLOWLY
BACK TO THE BOAT HOUSE

WHERE HOPKINSON

THE HEAD CHEF

IS CONDUCTING A SERIES

OF CULINARY EXPERIMENTS

USING A REVOLUTIONARY

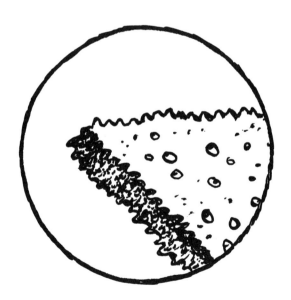

NEW FORM OF POLENTA.

WITH THE PRESSING MATTER OF
THE NEXT MEETING OF THE
CROCHET SOCIETY WEIGHING
HEAVILY ON HER MIND, LADY
BARTLEY SLIPS OUT OF
SAN FRANCISCO,

UNAWARE THAT SHE IS BEING FOLLOWED

BY A KEY MEMBER OF AN ÉLITE INTERNATIONAL SURVEILLANCE SQUAD.

DAGMAR BIENOWSKI FINDS HIMSELF
OUTSIDE A LOG CABIN IN ARIZONA

...ALTHOUGH HE HAS NO RECOLLECTION

OF EVER LEAVING ENGLAND.

BACK HOME, LAZENBY IS DEEPLY
CONCERNED. MEDIA SPECULATION
IS INTENSE. HIS OFFICE IS
BOMBARDED WITH TELEPHONE
CALLS NIGHT AND DAY. WITH
THE SITUATION RAPIDLY
BECOMING UNBEARABLE, HE
DECIDES TO RIDE OUT THE
STORM IN THE ONLY WAY HE
KNOWS HOW.

YET LESS THAN THREE MILES AWAY

THERE IS AN INTOXICATING

AIR OF UNBRIDLED HEDONISM
SWEEPING THROUGH THE
ENTIRE LAZENBY HOUSEHOLD.

A SERIOUSLY DIMINISHED AND
DAZED BIENOWSKI IS ROUNDED
UP AND BROUGHT IN FOR

QUESTIONING IN YUMA.

UP ON THE ROOF OF BROGDALE

LODGE, A NEW DISH IS ADDED TO THE LUNCHTIME MENU.

OFF THE COAST OF HAWAII
LADY BARTLEY HAS MANAGED
TO SECURE A PLACE AT THE
CAPTAIN'S TABLE WHERE, SHORTLY
AFTER DOWNING A LARGE COCKTAIL,

SHE OFFERS HIM A GOLDEN

OPPORTUNITY TO INVEST IN HER
IMITATION JADE BUDDHA IMPORT-
EXPORT BUSINESS.
WHEN HE DECLINES, SHE STORMS
OUT, JUMPS SHIP IN HONOLULU,
PURCHASES A GREEN PLASTIC
UKELELE ON THE QUAYSIDE AND
MAKES A TELEPHONE CALL TO
HOPKINSON'S KITCHEN AT BROGDALE
LODGE.
WHEN P.C. FENTON ANSWERS, SHE
DROPS THE UKELELE, REPLACES
THE RECEIVER AND HEADS OUT
TO THE AIRPORT.

AS LUNCHTIME APPROACHES, LAZENBY
IS HANDED A SLICE OF PIZZA AND
A CUP OF TEA AND THE NEWS THAT

LADY BARTLEY HAS GIVEN THE
SURVEILLANCE TEAM THE SLIP
JUST SOUTH OF SAN DIEGO.

FOLLOWING UP ON A LEAD FROM
ANTIQUES DEALER ARBUTHNOT,
LIEUTENANT MOCHALSKI HAS
TRACKED DOWN LUCY HENDERSON
AT A SUET RECYCLING FACILITY
IN NEW JERSEY.

THE BUILDING IS SURROUNDED
AND THE SUSPECT IS SOON IN
HAND CUFFS, HEADING DOWNTOWN,
PROTESTING HER INNOCENCE.

BACK AT Nº 27 RUTLEY CLOSE,
SIGNS OF STRESS ARE BEGINNING
TO SHOW.

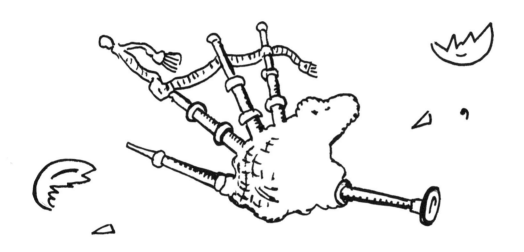

DOROTHY LAZENBY IS FILING
FOR DIVORCE ON GROUNDS OF
IRRECONCILABLE DIFFERENCES.

DAGMAR BIENOWSKI IS SENT

BACK TO ENGLAND

AND THE TROUBLED LAZENBY
RECONSIDERS HIS POSITION.

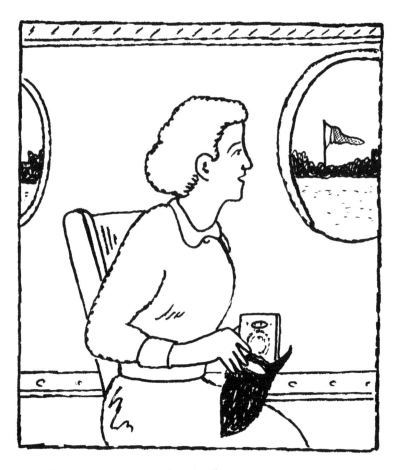

LADY BARTLEY ARRIVES IN PARIS
WITH A FALSE PASSPORT AND BEARD.
TWO HOURS LATER SHE IS SITTING
IN A CHARTERED TWIN-ENGINE
PLANE, TAXIING DOWN THE RUNWAY
ON HER WAY TO BROGDALE LODGE.

AS LAZENBY PRISES HIMSELF
FROM THE BRANCHES, A
REPORT FROM THE BANGKOK
POLICE DEPARTMENT LANDS
ON HIS DESK

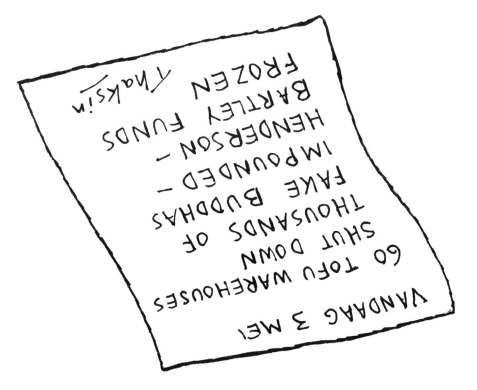

IN FRONT OF AN ASTONISHED CROWD

AT THE ORGANIC BLUEBERRY
YOGHURT COUNTER IN A SAN
FRANCISCO SHOPPING MALL,
LOUIS BRADLEY IS ABOUT TO
PLAY "SOMEWHERE OVER THE
RAINBOW" ON HIS ACCORDION
WHEN HE SPONTANEOUSLY
COMBUSTS, LEAVING ONLY
A PAIR OF SMOKING BROGUES

TO REMIND THEM OF WHAT
MIGHT HAVE BEEN.

AFTER RECEIVING A NUMBER
OF DEATH THREATS SIGNED,

LAZENBY EMPLOYS THE SERVICES
OF A BODY DOUBLE AND IS ADVISED
BY HIS DOCTOR TO TAKE A FEW
DAYS' UNPAID LEAVE.

HE IS RELAXING AT HOME
WATCHING A PORNOGRAPHIC DVD
WHEN THE TELEPHONE RINGS.

IT IS "WOBBLY" WILKINS WITH
NEWS OF LUCY HENDERSON'S
ARREST AND EXTRADITION.
"ANY NEWS OF HER PARTNER
THE ELUSIVE LADY BARTLEY?"
SNAPS LAZENBY AS HE
JUMPS UP, DISLODGING THE
FAMILY HEIRLOOM.

AT A HIGH SECURITY SURVEILLANCE
POST JUST SOUTH OF GUILDFORD

DESPERATE ATTEMPTS TO LOCATE
LADY BARTLEY ARE UNDER WAY.

TWENTY MINUTES LATER, RICHARD
CHAMBERLAIN, A RETIRED FLORIST,
IS TENDING HIS SNAPDRAGONS IN
THE GARDEN OF HIS BUNGALOW
ON THE EDGE OF DRINGEMOOR.
HEARING THE DRONE OF A
LIGHT AIRCRAFT HE LOOKS UP
AND SEES THE FIGURE OF LADY
BARTLEY

DRIFTING SLOWLY DOWN TO EARTH.

P.C. WILKINS IS DISPATCHED TO BROGDALE LODGE...

WHERE HOPKINSON IS DEALING

WITH ANOTHER CUSTOMER COMPLAINT.

LAZENBY'S BODY DOUBLE

NARROWLY SURVIVES AN ATTEMPT
ON HIS LIFE IN THE CAR PARK
OF THE GUILDFORD AND DISTRICT
TAXIDERMY SHOWROOMS.

A STRUGGLING LUCY HENDERSON

LANDS AT SOUTHAMPTON DOCKS.

YET LAZENBY REMAINS A TROUBLED
MAN. LADY BARTLEY IS STILL ON
THE LOOSE AND REPORTS OF

MYSTERIOUS ACCIDENTS CONTINUE
TO FLOOD IN FROM A NUMBER OF
LOCATIONS AROUND THE GLOBE.

GUILDFORD REACHES BOILING POINT.

THERE IS, HOWEVER, REASSURING
NEWS FROM BANGKOK, WHERE
NAKON THAKSIN HAS COMPILED
AN IMPRESSIVE DOSSIER ON

THE CRIMINAL ACTIVITIES OF THE
BARTLEY-HENDERSON EXPORT
OPERATION, OUTLINING DETAILS
OF MASSIVE CORPORATE FRAUD,
INSIDER DEALING, SMUGGLING FAKE
ARTEFACTS AND TOFU LAUNDERING
ON AN INTERNATIONAL SCALE.

LAZENBY HURRIES DOWN TO JOIN
WILKINS AT BROGDALE LODGE.
TOGETHER THEY SEARCH THE
BOATHOUSE. WILKINS WOBBLES
FORWARD, STOOPS, AND PICKS UP
A SHEET OF PAPER.

WIND-DRIED TOFU
ON A BED OF
WILTED KALE,
SERVED WITH A
GARNISH OF CHILLI
& CORIANDER SUET

"WHAT'S THIS?" HE ASKS
"I'M AFRAID IT MAY WELL BE A
RECIPE, WILKINS" REPLIES HIS
SUPERIOR SOMEWHAT GRAVELY.

LESS THAN HALF A MILE AWAY
HOPKINSON IS TRYING DESPERATELY
TO CONTACT THE CENTRAL TOFU
WAREHOUSE IN THAILAND

WHILST LADY BARTLEY IS IN THE BROGDALE KITCHENS

HIDING HER PARACHUTE IN ONE OF HOPKINSON'S MOUSSAKAS.

EIGHT MINUTES LATER
A POWERFUL EXPLOSION ROCKS
THE LODGE,

FOLLOWED BY THE SOUND
OF BAGPIPES

AND THE SLAP OF WRISTS
ON LEATHER.

WHEN THE SMOKE CLEARS HOPKINSON IS CORNERED.

LADY BARTLEY'S ATTEMPT TO FLEE IN A FLIMSY DISGUISE

NO HAWKERS

IS FOILED AND SHE IS QUICKLY OVERPOWERED, LEAVING OVER EIGHTY-SIX TULIPS AND A RECENTLY PLANTED EUPHORBIA BADLY TRAMPLED.

A TRIUMPHANT WILKINS EMERGES
FROM THE SMOKING RUBBLE AND
ANNOUNCES:

"I THINK I'VE FOUND CONCLUSIVE
EVIDENCE OF YODELLING, SIR."

THE TWO CULPRITS ARE BUNDLED
INTO A BULLET-PROOF VAN AND
WHISKED OFF TO A HIGH SECURITY
BUNKER ON THE OUTSKIRTS OF
MINCHINHAMPTON, WHERE THEY

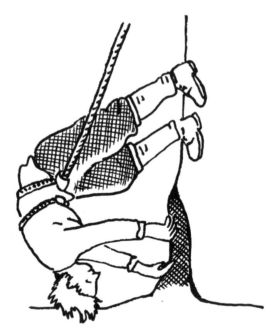

COME FACE TO FACE WITH LUCY
HENDERSON.

SHERIFF MᶜCULLOUGH AND HIS
DEPUTY UNEARTH A POWERFUL
RADIO TRANSMITTER AND A
CACHE OF ILLEGAL WIND
INSTRUMENTS.

AT THE SUBSEQUENT TRIAL, HENDERSON, BARTLEY AND HOPKINSON FACE A TOTAL OF 860 CHARGES, 17 OF WHICH ARE IN BREACH OF INTERNATIONAL TRADE AGREEMENTS.

THEY ARE SENTENCED TO 174 YEARS IN PRISON.

THE REMAINS OF BROGDALE
LODGE QUICKLY BECOME A

MAJOR TOURIST ATTRACTION.

PLANS FOR A TOFU EXPERIENCE THEME PARK ARE RUSHED THROUGH.

WILKINS IS PROMOTED. LAZENBY'S
DIVORCE BECOMES FINAL AND LEEDS
UNITED WIN AT ELLAND ROAD.
DAGMAR BIENOWSKI ARRIVES IN
PENZANCE HARBOUR, IS GREETED
LIKE A HERO AND GIVEN HIS
OWN SHOW ON RADIO CORNWALL:

"I PREDICT TOMORROW".

ELENA, LAZENBY'S EX-WIFE, ATTENDS A POLICE CHARITY BALL IN CIRENCESTER AND MEETS IRGOND, LAZENBY'S BODY DOUBLE IN THE CAR PARK.

TWO WEEKS LATER THEY ARE MARRIED.

NAKON THAKSON, CHAIRMAN OF THE
BOARD OF DIRECTORS OF ALLIED
TOFSUET INC., MOUNTS A
TAKEOVER BID FOR LEEDS UNITED F.C.

PLANS TO RELOCATE THE ELLAND
ROAD STADIUM IN CHIANG MAI
REACH A CRITICAL PHASE.

EIGHT YEARS LATER, SIX INCHES
ABOVE THE LAWN OF THE
FERNLEIGH RETIREMENT HOME
IN WIMBORNE, LAZENBY IS
RECITING A MANTRA

WHEN HIS INNER CALM IS
SHATTERED BY THE ARRIVAL
OF A POLICE HELICOPTER.
IT'S A VISIT BY DETECTIVE
SUPERINTENDENT WILKINS

BRINGING A LETTER FROM LADY
BARTLEY.

LAZENBY OPENS THE LETTER.
THE COLOUR DRAINS FROM HIS FACE
AND HE STARTS TO DRIFT SLOWLY

OVER THE TULIPS AND RAGWORT
TOWARDS LOWER DIMCHESTER.

AS HE FLOATS OVER THE VILLAGE
HALL HE HEARS THE OPENING
BARS OF "SOMEWHERE OVER
THE RAINBOW".
HE LOOKS DOWN

AND REALIZES THAT HIS TROUBLES
ARE JUST ABOUT TO BEGIN.

This laxe pith or marrow in man's head shows
no more capacity for thought than a cake of suet

HENRY MORE (1614—1687)

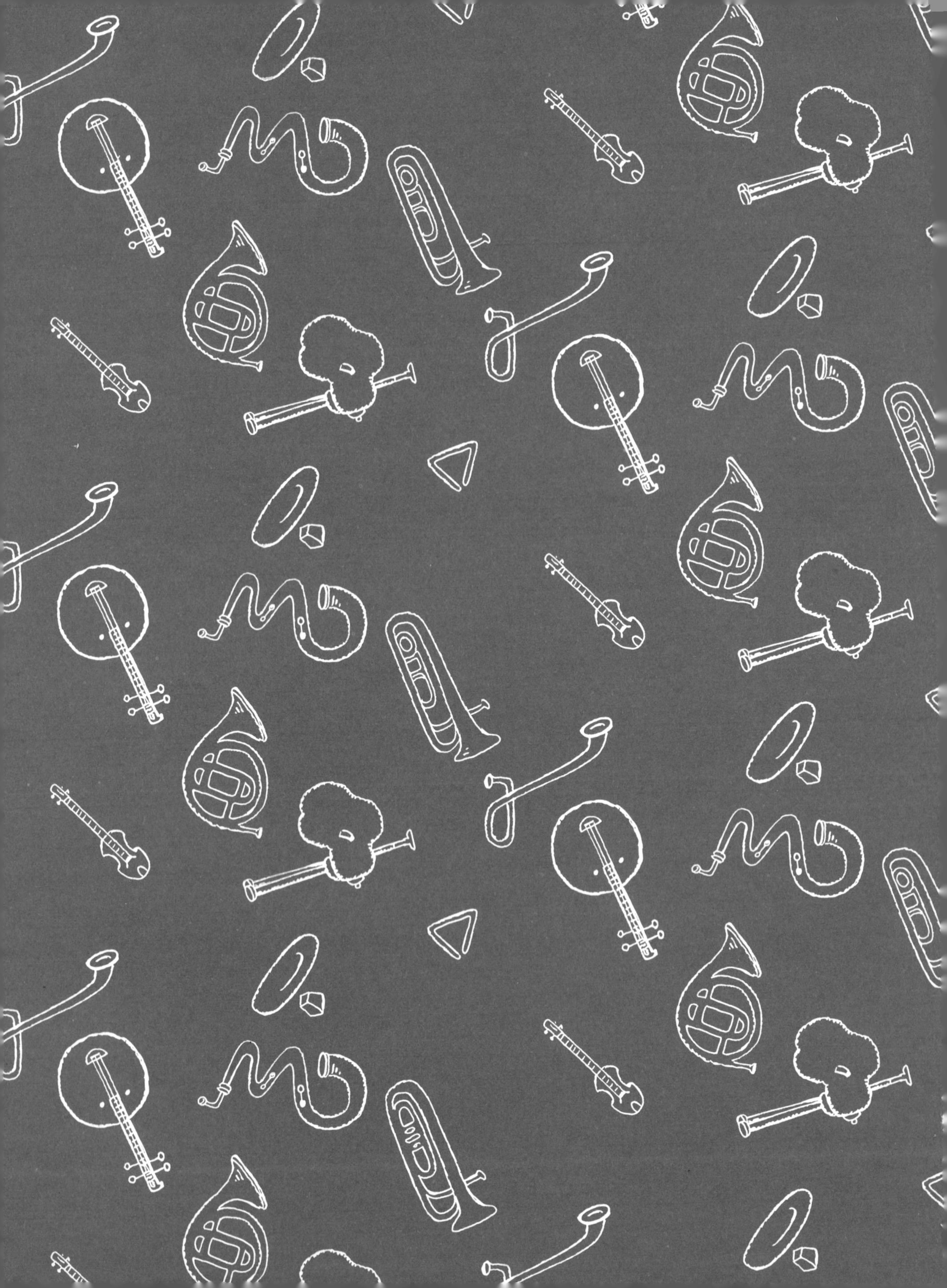